She's The Boss
Domestic violence against Men

By Timothy White, Sr.

She's the Boss © 2016 by Timothy White, Sr.

All rights reserved. Printed in the United States of America. No part of this book may be used or reproduced in any manner whatsoever without written permission except in the case of brief quotations embodied in critical articles or reviews.

This book is a work of non-fiction. However, names, characters, businesses, organizations, places, events and incidents either are the product of the author's imagination or are used fictitiously. Any resemblance to actual persons, living or dead, events, or locales is entirely coincidental.

For information contact:
info@uptownmediaventures.com

Book and Cover design by Tim White Publishing

ISBN: 978-1-68121-107-7

10 9 8 7 6 5 4 3 2 1

Table of Contents

Chapter	Page
Introduction	5
1. Happy Wife Happy Life?	7
2. I Don't Believe You	13
3. Surprise Surprise	25
4. Fate Worse Than Death	33
5. She's the Boss	45
6. Soul Mate to Hell Mate	53
Conclusion	61
About the Author	63

Introduction

When the conversation of domestic violence comes up, we immediately think about statistics that informs us of all the women who have been abused, or died due to abuse from men. Seldom do the conversations include the men who have been abused by women. This conversation often falls on deaf ears, and disbelief.

Men that are abused by women, are not talked about and when we hear that a man says he has been abused by a woman we tend to dismiss it as a joke, or it's impossible, because a man cannot be abused by a woman. Domestic violence is a double-sided coin, it doesn't only happen to women.

It may come as a surprise to some that there are many men being abused by their partners but seldom speak about it, and there are many reasons for this.

In the book, "In the ring with Heels on" the focus is on violence towards women, but the record has to be straighten out, and facts made known that there are women who also use violence as the way to get what they want from their partners. This book will introduce some to the hidden actions taken by some women. And bring to light for others the violence many men suffer in silence and shame, at the hands of the women they love.

Turning the light on for men to come out of the darkness is not an easy one, as their hurt is seen as wimpy and weak, and a real man takes care of business and rules his house.

The truth is not always flattering, and not always known, but in recent years it has become communicated through social media circles, and the secret is now out, and as unbelievable as domestic violence against men might seem, it's real, it's true and must be addressed.

Chapter 1
Happy Wife Happy Life?

This statement is used very regularly these days. I had never heard it spoken by anyone growing up. But for a new generation easily influenced, it's become the new rallying call for those who have married.

What does this statement mean and where did it come from? Some say it's a new take on, "if mamma ain't happy, nobody's happy".

Wherever it originated, it is not a realistic view of what a relationship is to be built on. It puts the power of everything going on in the relationship on how the woman feels, or is treated, and if she is not happy, then nobody's going to be happy.

Strange we never hear, "Happy husband happy home", is there one standard for women and another for men when it comes to happiness?

This thinking is dysfunctional at best as it places the happiness of all those in the relationship on what the husband does to make his partner happy.

The man's sole responsibility according to this statement is to be focused on the woman and her happiness requirement if he or anyone else is to be happy.

Happiness is a choice

Happiness is not guaranteed no matter what is done, if that happiness depends on an outside source to secure it.

In marriage, an individual's own mental and emotional state is the best indicator of whether their relationship will work or falter.

But, if or when a relationship does not work, or is not working, blame has to be affixed to someone, and in this case it's the man who is guilty of neglect, emotionally and possibly physically.

When a statement such as "he does not do the things he used to," to MAKE ME HAPPY is spoken, it suggest that the man is lacking in his duty to see, and focus on the woman's exclusive joy. If this is not done as she expects in her mind, he must be giving this attention to another woman, and must be unfaithful to her.

Does "happy wife" mean it's okay to have a "miserable man", since his happiness is not as important as hers?

For many women this is where their relationship begins and falls apart, it's all about what the man does, how he makes them feel, and what he does to keep that feeling alive.

The standard for the woman becomes her happiness almost exclusively, with a hint of "if I'm happy he is happy too". Nothing could be further from the truth.

I wanted to research this statement, "happy wife happy life" and found that Google has almost 5 million results, which suggest that this has become a large part of the thinking process for many women in relationships, as the formula for their happiness.

Relationships involves two people, not only one. Happiness is determined by two people not one, and based on individual choices that are made that includes them both.

Relationships depend on the power of two, not the dominance of one

What happens when a man does not give all his complete attention to his wife, or girlfriend, and what happens if she does not believe he is doing what she believes it takes to make and keep her happy? Discord erupts.

Relationships require that there be good communication, not forced understanding if they are to work together with efficiency.

Maybe this thinking is simply a revision from, "The hand the rocks the cradle rules the world". This is considered a powerful statement because it suggest that the woman has the greatest influences on a child as she is the one who spends the most time with them from the womb to adulthood.

So, how does this tie into domestic violence? Violence, domestic or otherwise is about getting what the predator desires, and to make them happy is to secure happiness, controlled by them for everyone around them.

Not everyone will agree with the thinking that making the woman happy is the door to family happiness and we will look at some of the dangers that comes about when the man, given time does not make, or pursuit making his partner happy.

Over the years I have witnessed, and spoken to men who were being abused emotionally, and physically, just like women, and who have suffered at the hands of their partners.

The major difference now being, that when men are abused, it's rarely believed as we will talk about later.

Part of the problem men endure, is that of emotional need, security and comfort.

Pay close attention, LOVE is not mentioned as it rates low and sometimes last when compared to what most women seek in a relationship.

She's the Boss

Happy wife is a term that carries little merit as it is not the goal of the man to make or keep a woman happy.

The danger comes from a woman embracing suspicion, jealousy, and distrust that comes from personal insecurity, and emotional distress, based on what someone does or need to do that brings them happiness.

Emotional distress can lead to physical violence, triggered by thoughts of being neglected, or rejected brought about by feelings of not being made happy.

Happiness is often based on feelings, not facts, it's based on how the other party made us feel, the excitement of feeling complete, and making them laugh, and feel special.

When these emotions are experienced, no one wants to lose it, but it must also be said, that these feelings are already inside, all that's missing is the willingness to revive and explore them.

Timothy White, Sr.

Chapter 2
I Don't Believe You

One of the hardest things to convince most people of is the fact that men can be victims of domestic violence. When we hear of domestic violence we don't think of men as victims, but rather perpetrators of it.

What makes this even more disconcerting is the fact that no one believes it takes place, or how can a woman be a predator.

When police are called to a home where there is a domestic dispute, they seem to automatically assume the guilty party is the man, especially when there are acts of violence, cuts and bruises.

When a man seeks to defend himself verbally,

and sometimes physically it's automatically seen as an admission of guilt.

Perception is not always factual. There are statistics that bear this out.

There are women who take advantage of the fact they are in a relationship that their partner does not believe in putting their hands on them to cause them physical harm.

Domestic violence against men is not always easy to identify, but it's become a serious threat, and can lead to harm or death.

We will be talking about ways to know and recognize if you're being abused, and sometimes it could require outside help to end it. But men do not often seek it.

Just like women who suffer from domestic violence, there are men that do not see they are being abused, most often on the emotional than physical level, but this can include sexual abuse and threats.

It's not uncommon for the woman to get in her partners face and yell at them, poking them with their finger, or even pushing them, and these little actions can be seen as early indicators of what is to come.

Women are encouraged to seek help, and to tell someone what has taken place. Men are told to simply forget about it, that men are strong, and if word got out what will others think about them? Abused men can be taunted by other men saying things such as "You're a man don't let her hit you without hitting her back", " you have to be kidding", or "you're joking right"?

A man will feel he is sometimes less than a man because he allows a woman to abuse him, he will hide this fact, and some decide to hit back (*this is discussed more in the book "In the ring with Heels on"*).

Those men who don't defend themselves are thought to be less manly, and cowards by some of their friends who are not afraid to let them know how they personally feel.

So what is a non-violent man to do? He either takes the abuse or seeks help, and gets out of the relationship before further harm can be done to him.

Or, is he to remain in a relationship surrounded by disrespect, and violence to show his love for his abuser?

Relationships are like babies, they are not what they will become and we must be careful to feed them correctly with the nourishment they require to grow healthy mentally, emotionally as well as spiritually.

Relationships are time sensitive as the process of development is as much observation as it is implementation.

When a man is perceived to be weak emotionally, then he is taken advantage of, if he was taught to respect women verbally and physically it can be seen as an opportunity for some women to abuse him because of his kind nature.

Domestic violence follows a set pattern, going from threats to verbal abuse to physical violence

When there is police involvement it's not surprising that if there is violence in the relationship it is thought to be by the hands of the man and not the woman.

The numbers are staggering when you think about all the men who are in violent relationships, and secretly suffering domestic abuse by their partner.

She's the Boss

When it comes to domestic violence the man is always thought to be the aggressor, and seldom do men make the 911 call in the dispute even when they are being abused.

Fact: It has been shown that women who assault men are more likely to avoid being arrested than men who assault or defend themselves against a woman.

Women are seen by law enforcement and in the judicial system as the victims not the abusers.

Men delay calling the police because they fear no matter what they say they will be assumed the aggressor and be placed under arrest.

In a 1985 sample study of 41 homes by the National Family violence survey, it was found that where 1 to 10 calls to the police had been made the following took place.

The breakdown was as follows, 24 female callers and 17 male callers. It was found that when a woman called the police to report domestic violence, the man was ordered out of the house in 41.4% of the cases.

However, when the man called the police, the woman was ordered out of the house in 0% of the cases.

When a woman called the police, the man was threatened with arrest immediately in 28.2% of the cases.

When a man called the police, the woman was threatened with arrest in 0% of the cases.

When a woman called the police, the man was threatened with arrest even at a later date in 10.7% of cases.

When a man called the police, the woman was threatened with arrest at a later date in 0% of the cases.

When a woman called, the man was arrested in 15.2% of the cases.

When a man called, the woman was arrested in 0% of the cases.

In fact, stats show in 12.1% of cases where the man called the police and they arrived, the man himself was arrested, even though he made the call.

I don't believe you. No matter what takes place the man is assumed guilty.

A True Story

Given by Ethan September 12, 2014

As a boy I watched my father physically assault my mother, the most scarring was when he choked her until she passed out.

As I got older I always knew that I would never be like him. I was never very tall but I was always very strong and muscular and was very aware of the type of violence I was capable of.

My first love Jenny was my world, she convinced me to leave the Bronx which was where I grew up and all of my family was. When we moved to her home town things were great, we were young and in love, the sky was the limit he thought.

After a while the truth about who she was began to surface. It began with belittling comments, and gradually escalated to days and nights of me worrying about what she was going to do next.

She would throw things at me, curse at me, emasculate me, slap and punch me and by the end, she threatened me, with and tried to use a knife to cut me.

I was holding my oldest son and she came out of the kitchen with a knife in her hands saying that she was tired of me and that since I won't take a hint and leave she will just have to make me leave.

Timothy White, Sr.

I thought at first that she was kidding, but then she lashed out at me with the knife.

I couldn't believe that she tried to cut me while I had my son in my arms; I put my son down, grabbed her, and pushed her against the wall all the while she's swinging the knife.

I was eventually able to get the knife from her but that wasn't until I grabbed her by the neck with the hand that was not restraining the hand with the knife and began to squeeze.

She dropped the knife and it took me a second to let go, I was angry, not just because she tried to cut me while I was holding our son in my arms but also because she turned me into a man that I did not want to be, my father.

I let her go, packed a bag, kissed my son good bye and left. I didn't have anywhere to go or stay and was sent into a depressive tail spin.

It took me many years to recover from that, to realize that I wasn't my father and that what I did, I did in self-defense.

I didn't know it when it was happening but she was abusing me, mentally, emotionally and physically.

I once told this story to a friend of mine in confidence, his question was why didn't I kick her ass, and why was I being such a bitch about it.

This is the truth behind a man being the victim of domestic abuse. The shame of being a man and being in that type of situation is soul crushing.

Men being victims of domestic violence is a dirty secret that most men will not admit to.

Even though I have come to terms with it I still can't talk about it, so much so that I didn't use my real name for this post. I am an almost 50 year old man that is so scarred by what happened to me that I can't be in a relationship, so much so that I am still single.

While I was in the military there was a guy I worked with that lost his home, money and eventually his life because he was in a similar situation.

One day he comes to the command and requests a cool down room because he and his wife had gotten into a fight.

The police came to the base and arrested him

because his wife called, and said that he had hit her. He admitted to hitting her, but only to get away because she had attacked him.

A couple of days later he was released on bond and was not allowed to leave post.

That night he committed suicide, a few weeks later my unit was called to muster.

Our commanding officer told us what happened, and the results of his autopsy.

It was found that he had scratches over most of his neck and back, he had old, and new bruises, and worst of all, he had suffered a severe blow to his groin, which was swollen and he had suffered a testicular rupture.

He had left a note, and in it he talked about how he had told the police about what she had done, and that they said that he was just making it up so that he wouldn't go to jail.

He said how one of the officers went as far as to suggest that he had someone purposely caused his injuries, so that he could say his wife did it.

The interviewing officer asked him how he expected them to believe his story when his wife was barely over 5 feet tall, and skinny as a rail.

He said it was because he refused to fight back, the cops reply was to taunt him, by pretending to be crying, and saying boo hoo, my wife hit me.

The shame of admitting that he, the man, was a victim of abuse and then suffering the taunts and humiliation by the police, losing his home, and everything else, left him feeling that there was nothing left but to commit suicide.

He was over 6 foot tall, 200 plus pounds and extremely athletic. Because of his stature, and job no one would believe him, this is the nasty truth about this type of abuse and why it does not get reported.

Men are always looked at as the perpetrators, even when they react in self-defense. We need to open up about this, we need a safe place to be able to open up about this, because if I can go through it and he can go through it, there is no telling how many others out there are in the same situation or have been, and already have taken their lives over it.

When a man hits a woman, the woman is a victim, when men hit women and the woman fights back, the woman is the victim, when a woman hits a man, very few people believe or acknowledge his situation, and go out of their way to avoid calling him a victim but rather the abuser.

When a woman hits a man and a man defends himself, the woman becomes the victim.

The percentage of women that commit domestic violence has almost equaled that of men that batter women, yet the legal system prosecutes less than 10 percent of women as compared to the 80 plus percent of men.

It's very disturbing that women can commit domestic abuse, and rarely are they charged. Just because we are men does not mean we are any less a victim, where are the man's rights?

When it comes to domestic violence, neither size nor gender matters.

Chapter 3
Surprise Surprise

When it comes to domestic violence it does not come to the surface immediately. It is generally gradual, very slow and almost unnoticeable, it's like a  coiled snake waiting for the best moment to attack, and it appears to have come from nowhere. The truth is, the tendency towards violence was always there, and simply needed a trigger, and we will look at some of the things that are potential violent triggers.

Men who are searching for love can find themselves drawn to and seduced by a physical relationships and outward beauty and not know the true person hiding beneath that outward image.

Often the violent attacks begin simple, just little things that are quickly ignored but in time escalate to dangerous levels.

For instance, sarcasm, a seemingly innocent push or verbal shove, something said to hurt emotionally and get a negative reaction, said almost jokingly but sincerely, and this over time leads to the elevation of voice to shouting and eventually screaming.

As men we are taught to be in control of our lives, and that we have the ability to overcome situations that confronts us.

But we are not taught what to do when we come across women that are manipulators and deceivers. Some men see this as a good thing that the woman is thought to be individually strong, and independent, and can stand up for herself.

To be assertive is not something negative, but can become so, in how and when this assertion is projected to others.

For many of us we say we don't want any surprises as we enter relationships, but at the same time we are not careful when entering relationships.

A couple of statements that has been heard is, "You really don't know me", and "you have no idea what I'm capable of doing". The surprise is not that these things are said, but, when they are said. Usually times of anger.

They are often made in the heat of disagreements and are punctuated by emotion.

For many of us we see this as "the getting to know you stage", and we accept the apologies made, and for the most part think nothing more of it.

"She would never do a thing like that", "it's not in her", and "she wouldn't hurt a fly".

Take the following old sayings that have been placed in our subconscious for example, that little girls are made of "sugar and spice and all that is nice" and little boys are made of, "snaps and snails and puppy dogs tails".

Are these statements true, of course not but they have been perpetuated?

The internet is filled with women who have no shame in saying what they will do to someone if they get, (*often assumed*), hurt by a man. WE'RE NOT GONNA TAKE IT ANYMORE.

When there are acts of aggression, many of us act stunned, shocked and amazed, but it's been all around us and presented to us all along, it's advertised and promoted through moral decay. It's "a dog eat dog world", me verses them, the strong verses the weak, and winners and losers we are told.

Revenge has become something we now call sweet. It's sought at any cost as long as there is the satisfaction of accomplishment accompanying it.

Jealousy is the forerunner to revenge, no surprise there.

If a woman can come across to others as weak

and a damsel in distress more people will come to her rescue as she is seen as helpless and in danger.

We seem startled and amazed when we learn that the person we believed we were happily linked and associated with turns on us, when it was simply a matter of objective observations overlooked. Are you really surprised?

What does this mean? There's nothing technical here, just simple observations that can easily be learned by having a watchful eye and open ears. Women are as dangerous as men when it comes to dishing out hurt and pain.

The biggest surprise comes when we finally acknowledge that we cannot change people and make them become what we want them to be, as it is human nature to resist and rebel.

It's akin to training a lion to do tricks. Yes, we can train a lion, but it is never tame. It remains a lion and when the time is right its instincts kick in and it will do what a lion will do, ATTACK.

Not being prepared is to be willingly blind to reality.

When there is no solidarity in a relationship, no working together, no singleness of direction, there will certainly be hostility on the horizon.

Women seek power just as men do, and it should not come as a surprise when they do.

Women, like men, want to be seen as valuable, and contributors, beginning at home, and just as men can be corrupted by power, so also can women.

It should be understood that not one of us is what we appear to be on the surface.

The body is merely the external covering to what's unseen, hidden and developing inside.

An amazingly beautiful car on the surface might look great upon first inspection but can be found in horrible condition under the hood and elsewhere because a thorough examination was not conducted because of emotion and the adrenalin of want.

Still, one of the hardest things to admit is that of making a mistake, to say we made a bad decision.

A house can be beautiful outside and yet be missing all the material needed to complete the interior. Time and commitment are requirements needed to build the home or car into what they should be, bear in mind also that the car and the home are material things, people are not. We can add to what is already considered essentially complete.

Relationships require that we pay close attention, relationships don't just happen, they are works in progress.

In the development of a relationship both parties already have agendas, and what they are looking for, and expect from this union.

The biggest surprise is when they (the abuser) discover things are not going as they anticipated, and so begins the conflict, and slowly revealing their true nature.

It becomes time to show who's really running things and who's actually in charge.

Are these acts truly surprising, not altogether?

When we take the time to step back and examine things carefully, it becomes clear what we potentially have to face, if we continue in the specified direction we have chosen.

We are not (or should not be) looking for a PERFECT RELATIONSHIP, as there are none. But it's possible to have a good working relationship based on moral values and personal respect.

The majority of abuse begins simple enough, it starts out on the emotional level and often ends with physical abuse.

The only real surprise sometimes is how quickly it might escalate from one level to the other.

Abusers know they are so. They enter into relationships seeking the power to control others from the start, and they will fish until they get a bite emotionally, and will do whatever they have to, and play whatever game is effective to get their desires met, including the use of fear, intimidation, and the use of violence.

Chapter 4
Fate Worse Than Death

There are things worse than death we are told. I can ruin your life without putting my hands on you. The police will believe me before they believe you. The court is own my side.

They, (*the children*) will say whatever I tell them to say.

These are only a few statements that have been made to men over the years, when a partnership or relationship comes to an end, and she refuses to let him go, or move on with her life.

Some things appear to be worse than death, as death is seen to be the end of all things, particularly suffering. Death is preferred rather than suffering.

Pictured here is Simon Kiguta who in 2012 had his face slashed by his wife Julianna for coming home drunk and wanted to go to bed. Suffering, (or discomfort), is a natural and sometimes unavoidable part of life.

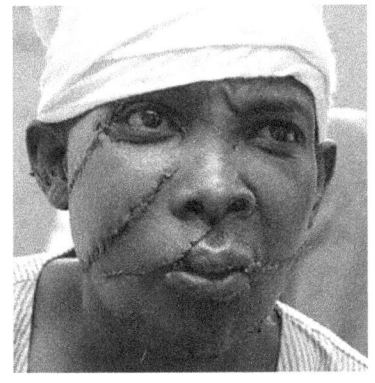

Everything in life serves a purpose, and can be viewed from one of two perspectives, **1)** negative or **2)** positive.

Many events take place in our lives that we have no control over, some that are seen as negative, such as storms, rain, hurricanes, floods, loss of jobs and maybe health.

We don't control the weather, and jobs can be lost due to any number of circumstances, and our health is not assured, as accidents can befall us at any moment.

But, there are a few things that we do have control over, and that is, how we respond to the events as they unfold in our lives.

We've seen how people responded to hurricanes and floods around the world.

How do positive people in spite of their situations still see the glass as half full rather than half empty? They realize that as long as they have life, they could put physical things back together again over time.

Negative people, however, only see a life disrupted and inconvenienced with things brought about by what someone else has done, and they now live in pain, and remain in the pain of despair, presumably because of others.

These women, who like Julianna, are angry for what has HAPPENED TO THEM, and they take things personally even blaming God and some even questioning his existence because of what they have experienced.

People are generally happy when ALL IS WELL WITH THEM, when the world seems to revolve around them, their ideals, and their wants.

To live with less is an insult to them, it's a poverty mentality.

Every human being seeks to be comfortable, and secure, and want for nothing.

Men and women seeking the companionship of a relationship are no different. We find at life's center is security, being comfortable, and surprisingly not love.

Relationships should be focused around compatibility, and spiritual commonality, especially for those who make a boast of seeking their soul mate.

So, what happens when the individual is determined not to be "the one", and when everything believed to be true is not what was expected?

Many relationships are known from the

beginning, we have called these "red flag" moments. Moments that the true person's attitude, personality, and demeanor are clearly seen, but ignore, and overshadowed for want and desire.

Both women and men are guilty of this thinking, as everyone wants to be happy, not so much within themselves, but seeking to have their happiness like a fountain of compliments and encouragement flowing to them from someone else.

The majority of relationships are based on what the other person can do for them, and not what they can do for themselves.

With that being said, it becomes abundantly clear to anyone wanting to know the truth, why failures seem to out-weigh successes when it comes to relationships.

As we have mentioned, many relationships are not about love, but security, financial security to be more precise, and those in relationships value that more than anything else.

So, when it comes to hurt, it also becomes clear, that in order to do the greatest harm to another person, you do it in what the world says **"hit them in the pocket book or wallet"**.

Financial destitution is one of the greatest types of suffering to one who has had a moderate, or comfortable lifestyle.

When it comes to domestic violence and abuse, this ranks high on the list.

Most people in relationships argue and fight over money or the lack thereof most often.

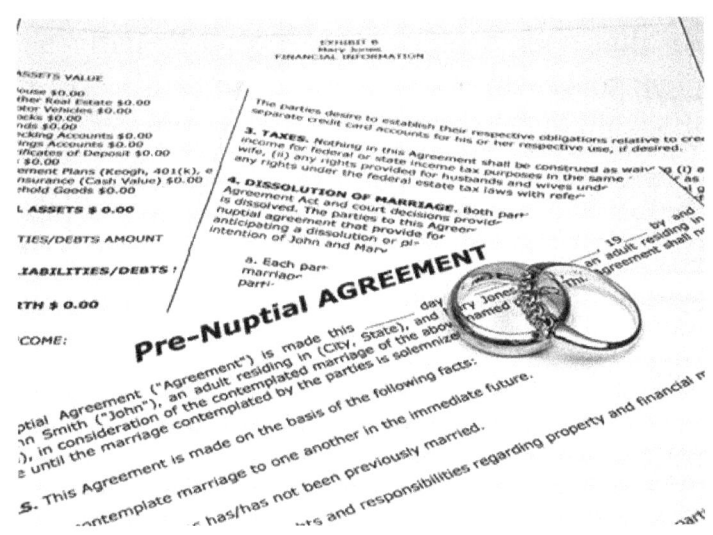

It's become normal to now before entering a relationship to have **a prenuptial agreement** made up in order to safeguard finances, and other personal assets from a partner, who might have grown accustomed to a certain lifestyle, and feels they are entitled to continue it at the expense of someone else.

It's the lavish lifestyle they seek, shoes, dresses, purses, nails, hair styles, and transportation once enjoyed, they are not willing to let it go, and some women will do whatever it takes to maintain it.

Certainly finances are needed to navigate through this life, but at what cost?

How far would someone be willing to go to obtain it or maintain it?

In this book we are speaking particularly about women and what some of them will do in a relationship to control it.

Some women, like men, were and are willing to cheat on their partners secretly, to enjoy the lifestyle they felt should be theirs.

Suffering physically, financially or emotionally consistently, and ongoing, is considered for some people, a fate worse than death.

Many of us have been brought up in a very material culture, and taught that "things" are representative of who we are, and a show of status, and being without these symbols, says to the world we are lesser in value to those who have more than us.

It's as much about ego, (and yes women have ego problems as well), as it is about abundance, and "look what I have."

Some women will and have resorted to deception

and violence to get what they want from a man, and were not opposed to lying to do so.

Some men resort to violence, if they feel attacked financially, and as we spoke about it in the book "In the ring with heels on"; these men have no problem with hurting anyone who they feel threatened by.

Then of course there are the men I speak about in this book, **men who instead of becoming violent become victims themselves**, of women who look at their gentle behavior as a weakness to be exploited.

There are men whose moral principles have not been corrupted, and so they are "taken advantage of.

A decent man is often victimized, because his thinking seems to be obtuse. He is not drawn to decision making by way of violence. And his meekness is seen as his weakness, because he is non-combative.

There are numerous men who have suffered at the hands of partners that saw them only for what they could give, or what they had. We have called women looking for these types of men "GOLD DIGGERS".

Men become victims because many of them think they could never become a victim, and they are too smart for that to happen to them.
For a man to be taken advantage of he feels shamed, embarrassed and hurt, the same feeling that

a woman feels when she believes she has been violated.

There are women who have exclaimed they have the power to make a man's life a LIVING HELL, and many of these women have no problem attempting to make that promise true.

Song upon songs are written to give encouragement to destructive behavior, such as "What's love got to do with it" and "When a woman's fed up", or "You can't raise a man".

Many of us have heard the saying "Hell has no fury like a woman scorned". These statements and others like them seem to suggest that negative actions are justified when someone is hurt in a relationship, and that lashing out is a remedy or coping cure.

Love and relationship is about your ability to trust the individual you have entered a relationship with.

But if that relationship is thought to have been violated the old saying, "the gloves have come off " is then applied, and there's a no holds barred mentality enacted, and it's now time to go for blood.

The goal is at this point, to cause as much suffering as humanly possible to the individual that is believed to have caused pain in their life.

Some women don't choose physical pain as a way

to get even, but will use financial pain as their weapon.

A woman does not do battle with a man pound for pound, she will often take another route, and that will be his road of ruin.

Some women will seek to ruin the man's life not in a (boxing) ring but through material things, or a wedding ring.

The wedding ring gives entitlement, and a legal course of action. It's becomes "what's yours is mine, and what's mine is mine". For many women it's the legal "I got you," if things go south.

There are countless men (and women) who have no knowledge of relationship building and therefore base their perception of a relationship on what they FEEL one should be like.

There is however some women who are not

opposed to physically attacking a man, especially those men who have not chosen to use violence as a way to communicate their displeasure or disagreement.

Physical abuse ranks high in the forms of disrespect, and is most often used when verbal and emotional abuse does not appear to work.

There are women who use violence as a crutch defense against a man, to ensure they will get the revenge they seek, if the man does not give them what they want. It's been a known fact that if the police are involved with a call of domestic violence it is commonly believed the man is the troublemaker and not the victim.

Consider the following statistics;

More than 830,000 men fall victim to domestic violence every year, which means every 37.8 seconds somewhere in the United States a man is battered.

Men who are usually battered by women are men who have had some history of abuse to their spouse verbally or physically, and in an act of revenge she strikes out against their attacker.

But, there are also women who verbally and physically abuse their partners who has never laid a hand on them. Women who are willing to make a false claim of such, even after they have physically attacked the man.

Chapter 5
She's the Boss

Strange as it might seem, there are women who like men want to be in complete and total control of what takes place not only in their life, but also in the lives of those around them.

What is it that makes a woman think she should be the controlling force in other people's lives? It's one thing to have control over the personal aspects of one's own life, but what is it that drives people to seek power over others?

Maybe it was the women suffrage movement which began around 1860, a time when women were viewed as lower class citizens and not on the same par or equal to men, when it came to voting, as they had no voting rights, or a voice, other than in the home as it pertains to children.

The woman's role was to please the man, to be OBEDIENT to him as her marriage vow has said, to love, honor and obey him.

Women, not all women, thought of themselves as lower than man (this did not include black women; they were seen as property not as people).

Maybe this new desire for freedom stems from women who sought to work rather than be homemakers, women who sought equal pay for equal work.

Certainly, there are any number of factors that could be named that might have some bearing on this mindset, and choice as to why a woman sought exclusive power over those in her life just like her male counterpart.

Is there anything wrong with a woman desiring life equality the same as a man? Absolutely not, but we are not talking about equality but power over other people.

This new mindset would later be seen in what was known as the Women Liberation Movement in the 1960's.

Many women are now seeking not only equal employment on the job, but to be the boss, the final voice in the decision-making process. A forceful, and demanding woman is no better than a forceful and demanding man.

A woman should know her place, and that place was in the home having a baby was the old adage.

This is not the thinking of the 20th century woman.

The old cigarette commercial of 1968 Virginia Slims (for women) advertised saying, "you've come a long way baby," "It's a woman thing" and "find your voice."

Women were seen as individuals for the pleasure of men; this however is no longer the case.

In days gone by when men would refer to their wives many would call them "the old ball and chain", which did not conjure up a picture of love and happiness.

The revolution through liberation was in full swing, and women would no longer be silent, and their voices would be heard.

Women as well as children have always been a part of the work world, but they were not often paid for their services as men, for the long hours they would put in. But that's for another book.

With freedom comes responsibility, not popularity. It's doing what is not always going to make friends, but it will remove barriers, and one of the greatest barriers is that of ignorance.

Although we have come a long way historically, there is still a long way to go when it comes to understanding the simple principles of what makes men and women different, and how these differences are helpful in our personal development, or destruction if not applied correctly.

When we abandon the ideals of value when it comes to others, the corrosion of our lives, and country takes hold, and books such as these are written.

"More" becomes the new battle cry, "it's not enough" and "I'm not satisfied" reverberates in the air.

When we abandon the moral, the immoral takes the stage, and its darkness claims the minds of many.

Needed change is not always received immediately, and treating anyone as lower class is not acceptable. We have labeled people as lower class, middle class, and wealthy as a way to define who is better or more important. This order of importance spills over into relationships as well. We have reset the morals bar and the standards are now low.

As women have come a long way they seek to have more materially and emotionally just as their male counterpart, and now we hear them say, "We're not going to take it anymore".

Sadly this also means they are now presenting actions and attitudes that men have demonstrated over hundreds of years, women have in effect learned (by example) that if you want something, you have to think, and do what men have done. It now means have no concern, show no pity, and have no compassion for anyone in your way as you move ahead in life, including a spouse or children. No one wants to be a slave in, or too, a relationship.

This at first might appear off subject, but it is in fact tightly wound into it. She's the boss, for many women springs from much of the history we mentioned here.

Remember, power corrupts, and absolute power corrupts absolutely, so we've been told, even the power we might seek to have in a relationship.

Freedom means liberty, and for many it means the ability to remove limits and restrictions. Women had found themselves in what can only be called FORCED SERVITUDE, and in the course of time and suffering, has now rejected it.

Women became stronger, and for many of them their wills became defiant. It was time to get their due and nothing was going to get in their way.

No longer having restrictions for home and having children as a way of life, the pressure is off, and now it's time to address the issue of who's the boss, and who's really in charge and running matters?

Many women have now become employers and bosses and where there are good employers, there are just as many if not more that are not.

The average man does not like to work for a woman, they feel it somehow makes them lesser of a man because a woman is telling them what to do. And there are some women who love this new position over men, and in some cases will abuse it even to the point of becoming threatening towards the man, if she is questioned.

When speaking to men concerning marriage it's not uncommon to hear the man say "she's the boss" when referring to their wives, or "I'm happy if she's happy."

It's being assumed that a man's happiness is dependent on whether or not the woman in the relationship is happy or not. She's the boss has even been heard being said when speaking of their relationship.

I have even seen shirts that reflect that statement. Am I saying women cannot or should not lead, absolutely not? There are many qualified women that are leaders in varying capacities. What I am referring to are those women who would do anything for total control in a relationship, and willing to use anything from threats to violence to ensure it.

Men must learn to be the leader in the relationship. Is this an insult to women, no, but it can be to those women that feel personally threatened.

When a man steps up to the plate of leadership, he understands this does not mean dictatorship, and getting results by force, but getting results by love.

Being the boss is not a positive thing. Its forcing specific wants and desires on another regardless to how the other party feels.

Anything said for a long period of time becomes

believable as well as acceptable. But it does not make it true.

Chapter 6
Soul Mate to Hell Mate

He's my soul mate, She's my soul mate, the love of my life, the ying to my yang, the light to my dark, the soft to my hard, the calm to my rage.

How often have you heard someone make one or more of these statements?

They say they had found their "Soul mate", the eternal love of their life.

But what some declare as a soul mate, is someone they simply are infatuated with, someone who makes them feel some kind of way.

There are many people that have made this boast but few actually live as though it is true, and there's a good reason for that as we will explore as we continue forward.

Soul mate meant something very different as I was growing up and the meaning has changed quite a bit over the years.

Soul mate is defined differently depending on the person you're talking to, who utters it, or believes it.

The before mentioned are a few definitions given for soul mate, that many of us have heard a soul mate to be.

This is a word that can stir people to action if nothing more than to argue their belief, and thoughts of what is meant by soul mate.

Of course, everyone wants to be happy, and to find happiness or something close to it, one would think they had found gold, but to find that elusive soul mate is to find someone more precious than diamonds or rubies.

For many of us we tend to look for love as the song put it "in all the wrong places," or settle for what we believe is love.

Here are two quick definitions for soul mate according to Merriam Webster: *1) a person who is perfectly suited to another in temperament and 2) a person who strongly resembles another in attitudes or beliefs.* Supposedly this word was first used in 1822.

But, we can trace it further back, in fact back biblically to the time of man and woman's creation.

 She's the Boss

We are told that man was created from the dust of the ground, And the Lord God formed man of the dust of the ground, and breathed into his nostrils the breath of life; and man became a living soul (Genesis.2: 7). and that man (Adam) should have a help meet(mate) someone for himself like all the other creatures.

So God created woman for man she was bone of his bone and flesh of his flesh (Genesis.2: 20-24).

In fact every woman according to the bible is a soul mate for someone. But this also means the two are to be compatible one with the other. There is someone for everyone, and **a soul mate does not mean a sexual bed buddy**.

A soul mate is someone you can be yourself with and share with, this can be a woman or a man. Love is not sexual it's spiritual.

Over 40 plus years I have spoken to countless individuals and it never ceases to amaze me how many people use the word soul mate when speaking of their relationship.

It's almost become a catch phrase to say they are complete and have found the person of their dreams. Dreams and reality are not the same, although we strive to make our dreams reality. Some of these same people who boast of finding their soul mate I have seen become bitter enemies later.

Those seeking relationships are looking for what they say is a soul mate, that individual who will complete the missing part of their lives, that individual to fill an emptiness, and void they had felt inside.

What many of them are actually seeking is an emotionally ongoing experience that will cater to their emotions, a relationship that will be focused on them at the exclusion of everyone and anyone else. Is this what a soul mate is?

Is a soul mate someone who threatens you with harm physically or otherwise?

Let's now take a closer look at some of the misdeeds done by some women who were first seen as caring, compassionate, thoughtful and loving people who at the flick of an emotional switch has moved from so called SOUL MATE to HELL MATE.

In order to move from one attitude to the other it's important that blame and fault is affixed to justify the accompanying actions.

Whatever the end result, it was due to the actions of the other person (soul mates) actions they brought on themselves.

Evil intent has to be rationalized and justified. Now you have heard me use the word evil for the first time in association with abuse. There is nothing cute or loving about the abuse of another human being.

Hell mate

So how does one go from being called a soul mate to becoming a Hell mate? What is a hell mate?

One becomes a hell mate when they have a status change; they are no longer seen as number one in the relationship and soon become emotionally distraught and fearful of personal economical or financial loss.

Violence is an act of fear, and we have been told "HELL has no fury like a woman scoured."

So what make someone go from soul mate to hell mate? Truth is, someone who is a true soul mate never becomes a hell mate.

A hell mate is driven by emotional despair and distrust, and believes they have been wronged and

Timothy White, Sr.

embarrassed and must take action.

A hell mate refuses to see any options other than those of hurt and harm, physical or financial.

Love is assumed to be real by how much someone has, the more they have in the relationship, the more they feel loved, and it's not keeping up with the Jones but being better than them.

A soul mate is not ownership or the property of a partner; it's not monitoring their every move, checking their phone, following them around, or fears them leaving your sight.

A soul mate is someone who works with you, and a hell mate someone working against you, and seeks to cause you harm.

A soul mate recognizes your needs as well as theirs, a hell mate sees only themselves as the important one in the relationship, and your happiness depends on them.

She's the boss. There are men living in fear of their partners and silently suffer from physical abuse, even justifying it as something that is accidental and not common to their relationship.

This is denial plain and simple, with a man secretly questioning his manhood and his leadership abilities.

When we doubt it leaves us open to being falsely led and dependent on feelings and not facts.

Relationships are not based on who's the boss, but there are some self-imposed limits applied that move the relationship forward.

For example, instead of becoming argumentative, and combative it's learning to understand the other person's position by good communication.

But what of those who no matter what you say, will oppose you at every hand, and sees you as being in the wrong?

Sadly this does occur, and there is not much you can do to help them cross that bridge, and if they're not open to seeking help, you then have to make a decision as to whether or not you want to continue to invest in a relationship that is not positive.

In any relationship the things done in them affect both parties.

Loud and vocal disagreements often slowly lead to verbal attacks that culminate in physical violence as well.

It's also important to know that we choose the kind of individuals we want to spend our lives with, but this is not always based on the fact we know, but the feelings we have about them.

Anger is an after effect of a situation that is not controlled by that individual's reasonable thinking, it's by someone who feels they have been wronged or taken advantage of. And of course, anger is often accompanied by revenge. Revenge does not consider how it will affect others; its focus is on bringing hurt to another who is believed to have caused them pain.

Conclusion

When it comes to domestic violence, we have been taught that women are the ones who suffer from it most and almost exclusively.

But the facts do not bear this out. There are thousands of men who have suffered from abuse and domestic violence at the hand of their spouses and girlfriends.

When it comes to men being abused, it is a conversation that is rarely spoken about. Men are abused, but it's kept very quiet by both men and women.

Men don't spend time talking about being physically abused as it is an embarrassment, and those who might find out about it might ridicule them and say they are weak and wimpy.

There are countless numbers of resources available for women who suffer abuse and places they can go for help.

This is not however the case when it comes to men. It's assumed that a man should be able to deal with a partner who has physically hurt them.

As there are emotional needs for a woman, the

same holds true for a man. Life is about balance, along with understanding life and relationships.

She's the boss shows how there is a danger when it comes to seeking dominance and control, and it doesn't matter if you are a woman or a man.

Myth, a woman cannot hurt a man by punching or hitting him. This book will help us to see the truth even if it is rejected. Even the myth of "Happy wife happy life."

About the Author

Timothy White Sr. has impacted thousands of people throughout the world as an author, teacher, motivational speaker and minister. Mr. White is on a mission to positively influence millions of people through his work, ministry and writing, which currently exceeds 80+ books covering a plethora of topics including bullying, domestic violence, self-help, history and spirituality.

The Cleveland, Ohio native, a father of five, has overcome many adversities in his life including homelessness and losing his beloved wife to cancer in 1994. Through much heartache and disappointments he discovered a new purpose and passion to use writing as a tool to "plant positive seeds."

Mr. White has developed profound spiritual insight into relationships over the years. Mr. White has written multiple books on the topic of abuse including, *In the Ring with Heels On*, *She's the Boss* and *Victims of Bullies*. Mr. White writes about these and other issues because of the relevance, and prevalence of domestic and other violence. He believes that, **"Information plus application equals transformation."**

Mr. White is an Evangelist and former pastor. He believes, "God chooses who He uses." He writes, speaks, and ministers to local, national, and international audiences. With an additional 15 new books in the works, Mr. White hopes to give people plenty of "spiritual food" to eat.

White is one of the producers of the documentary ***"Where's Gina?"*** about missing children on which he was also narrator.

He is a co-developer of a tech company (Gsys LLC) that brought blindside technology to vehicles that made billions for the industry, saving countless lives. He is currently co-hosting a radio show,

"Healing the Hurt" on WERE 1490am in Cleveland, Ohio on Thursday evenings 8-10 pm with Host, Rev. Brenda Ware-Abrams.

  He is currently on the Advisory Board and is a volunteer instructor at the Juvenile Correction centers in Warrensville Heights and Cleveland, Ohio where his book *Seven Signs of Success* is being taught. His book *Victims of Bullies* is, currently, in the City of Cleveland School system to help stop and make aware of solutions to the issue of bullying.

timwhite55@gmail.com Timwhitepublishing.com

www.ingramcontent.com/pod-product-compliance
Lightning Source LLC
Chambersburg PA
CBHW031256110426
42743CB00039B/613